The Navigators

Matthew Clegg
2017

The Navigators

Matthew Clegg

Longbarrow Press

Published in 2015 by
Longbarrow Press
76 Holme Lane
Sheffield
S6 4JW

www.longbarrowpress.com

Printed by T.J. International Ltd,
Padstow, Cornwall

ISBN 978-1-906175-26-9

First edition

Contents

9   *After Homer*

Trig Points

13   Redbreast
14   Outbreak
15   Frost Cure
16   Climbing to Another Climate
18   The Divers
19   Flight Path
20   Movements of War
22   Phineus
26   Kids of Wallsend
27   The Host
28   Treble
29   Speeches from *The Birds*
34   Shoal
35   The Tonic
36   The Lake in the Trees
37   Under Orion, Midsummer
38   Two Fugitives
39   The Tang
40   Punch
41   *Glad Tidings*
42   Trig Points
51   The Grate

The Navigators

55 The Sink Hole
56 Ballad of the Wandering Navvy
58 The Wheat Horse
59 Attercliffe
60 Harker's *Michael H*
61 Slow Days are Gone Days

63 In the 70s
64 Jasmine
68 Ellipses
69 The Passage

70 'Earthquake felt across much of UK…'
71 Winding Hole
72 Mexborough Quad Bandits
75 Canal Surf
76 Flood Risk
77 Brigand
78 Mexborough, Water-Fronted Properties Released
83 ANGLERS REQUIRE PERMITS
84 Mexborough Bridge S2
85 Darkhouse
86 The Edge
87 Dunn Street: Abandoned Lock
88 When They Next Make You Redundant
89 The Tug
90 Long Weeds

Cave Time and Sea Changes

93 Staithes
94 Our Love is a Whalebone
98 Counting Stones
103 Chalk
106 The Fates
108 Cave Time and Sea Changes

120 *After Apollonius*

123 *Afterword*
127 *Notes*
128 *Acknowledgements*

After Homer

Odysseus dug a trench,
                                   then poured offerings
    for the dead: sweet honey and milk, red wine,
water. He seasoned the mixture with barley,
    then he slit the tender throats of the lambs
over the trench, and let the dark blood curdle
    and cloud. The souls of the dead gathered there –
brides and grooms, unmarried men, old fathers
    and mothers, virgins longing to be kissed
and fighting men wearing spear-wounds like poppies.
    They came swarming around the reeking mull
like a rabble of dogs, mewling and keening
    for the blood that would give back taste,
                                   and speech.

Trig Points

'They hand in hand with wandering steps and slow
Through Eden took their solitary way.'

From *Paradise Lost*, Book XII, John Milton

'I cannot miss my way. I breathe again;
Trances of thought and mountings of the mind...'

from *The 1805 Prelude*, William Wordsworth

'Our life is looking forward or looking back. That's it.
Where's the moment?'

Ricky Roma, *Glengarry Glen Ross*, David Mamet

Redbreast

                              This is him,
                          rain-pecked
                  under a charcoal
          smear of cloud.
Watch him,
        moving
                in freeze-flames:
                        blood-breasted
                                feather-bauble –
                        pert beak,
                dainty feet –
        the bird in the bush
who won't
        come to hand.
                Wet wings of leaves
                        can't flit
                                like he does;
                        anatomies of ferns
                won't lift a frond.
        His accurate beak
nibs treble
        on treble,
                etching
                        and off-setting
                                his claim.

Outbreak

i.

The footpaths are closed.
A virus hitches on shoes;
  on the wind. We gaze
on fells eerily snow-glossed
and cleansed of all trace of us.

ii.

A line has been drawn
between man and beast. Cattle
  fuel the bonfires;
dioxins giving an edge
to smoke drifting into schools.

iii.

A coven of sheep
have strayed onto this A-road,
  hexing the traffic.
One driver nudges his horn
as a ewe licks a cat's-eye.

2001

Frost Cure

More subtle than snow
   and more delicate,
the bud
   on grass-blades
of silicon lilies.

Even sheep dung
   turns crystal
in sterilised light.

By the shore
   ice panes splinter
on reed stubble.

Peel one up
   and spin it
scatter-singing
   across the lake.

Kick-start your pulse.

Cough the spoor
   from your breath.

Climbing to Another Climate

Across the valley
the *Lion and Lamb*
free-floated on a carpet
of low-flying cloud
when the snow dropped.

> Each swarm of flakes
> was a magnified slow-mo
> of the particle world
> until we climbed
> into another climate
> where heartbeats steadied
> to the creep of sykes
> slowing down their pulse
> under ether of ice.

We glimpsed Windermere
drawing veils of mist
then trooped on
against gravity's bias
to attack the ridge.

> We made it up to Fairfield
> and there our story
> developed a stitch,
> got squeezed for breath.

On the summit
we freed gouts of steam
from our flasks
and lingered, gazing down
the snow-line, aghast
at the muscle tone
of drumlin, moraine –
　　　worked out
　　　over those seamless ages
　　　of taking the stress –
just about – under
a glacier's weight.

The Divers

Two divers
assemble kit
by the lake.
Tapping dials
and testing valves
they tune
into mist.
Sheathed against
cold shock
they plumb
roots
of Whin Rigg.
Imagine
those divers
as a banking jet
over-fills
the basin
with sonic burn.
In morphine dark
their out-breaths
hatch
through dense
ferment
of drone.

Flight Path

For Madeleine and Charlie

They hardly need us,
these fighters – their underwings
spiky with hardware,

louder than oceans –
scanners and tracking systems
de-bugged of feelings.

They scalp the trig points
as we scoop up small children.
Meant to protect us,

these heavies wipe out
the trebles of our season's
new lambs, almost snatch

birth cauls unfurling
from ewes, frenzying jackdaws
bunkered in chimneys.

Movements of War

i.

Peeling off the dressing from her cheek
she interrogates the mirror – falters

before smashing the glass. Beauty vanished
like the low swooping heron's reflection

as it plunges into itself.

ii.

Our own people drove us back with jeers, clubs.
separated from the tractors, I walked

without shoes towards the border at night:
I, an old man, who had never before

felt snails crunch under my flesh.

iii.

Rockets fall like festival streamers,
but the gunship holds position – hammers

its crude message. It is still spring here,
I tell myself. Yesterday I could've cried

for bees hovering as blossoms fell.

iv.

On these gusty days, when the sun is high,
it's harder to tell, without glasses,

if it's smoke-plumes or passing clouds
that send shadows shoaling over hills

caressing the contours like cruising jets.

v.

The food has gone, the babies crying –
so all of us ran to the relief trucks –

rich, poor – who never touched in the last life –
and there she was. What price on love, then,

in a scrum of grasping hands?

vi.

'What began in Kosova will end
in Kosova…' From this England

I listen for news of the K.L.A.
on the World Service. Even in my own

language, I'm slow to understand.

Phineus

i.

No-one's 'too big to fail.'
I'd been drinking hard
and woke with a rainbow bruise
on the bulge of my calf.
At the firm, email after email
drove a rod down my spine
and vision channel-hopped.
All my fingers missed their keys
and my lungs squeezed my heart.
I swayed to the window
as light and colour whitened,
crashing their edges to black.

ii.

I gave away
my library
out of spite,
but my ears
learned
audio books –
Homer
and Milton's
Paradise Lost.
I wasn't listening,
but seeing:
a blind man
given light
by blind men.

iii.

When a blind man panics
he can't flail his arms.
He must haul his breath
from the well of his gut
until the harpies in his ribs
stop flapping and clawing
and his fingers unfurl
spiders from his fists.

iv.

April on my skin
triggers
the laburnum
in my head.
The stems
are weighed
with petals
heavy as grapes,
so yellow,
each cup
brimming
with light
between clouds.

When I hear
kids swearing –
footballs
ringing hard
off walls –
I conjure
the laburnum.
Above fags
and beer cans,
the tips
of its stems
beckoning heat
to land
and ignite.

Kids of Wallsend

For Angela Hughes

Between shipyards
and newer factories
there's a path
of virgin tarmac
        sloping
a guillotine line
from Swan Hunter
to another yard
where ice melds
on nitrogen tanks
and the sagging wire
of an electric fence
nags the railings.
        This is where they play –
        the kids of graffiti-land:
they switch off *Call of Duty*
and bomb on scooters
down these runs –
        one leg frantic,
        the other yielding
        to absorb each jolt.
It's a long shot
those kids might look up
at cranes lifting
under their weight
and see them as they were –
        titans, saluting sky.

The Host
i.m. Robert Woof

Robert, were we reading Keats
    or Shelley
when you paused to tell
    how Ian McKellen
    had sat in your chair,
    lit a cigarette,
    then leant to exhale
    each drag
    up the chimney
    as if to whisper
    a secret pledge.

Our door was open
and bats snickered circuits
round your eaves.

    'A toad', you cooed,
    announcing its entry
    on the rug –

attentive
    even to toads.

Treble

From Townend,
Grasmere,
I'm on the phone
to Paul
in Kirkstall,
Leeds;
a coach
                reversing;
        birdsong
    piccolo sharp
from the phone;
all the birds
    of summer
held hostage
    in the wire;
            their calls
rinsing my ear
    with treble
            long after
        I clicked
                the handset
    dumb.

Speeches from *The Birds*
After Aristophanes

1. *Hoopoe's Cuckoo Song*

Billed quilled many feathered,
raiders of the farmer's furrows
liberating seeds and barley;
flocks and species in your millions;
cloud sopranos, hedgerow belters,
troubadours of rapeseed pastures
who will sing *jug jug, jug jug.*

Finches with bird-table manners,
coarse-tongued gulls at landfill banquets,
kestrels stuking on hard shoulders,
peeling roadkill off the fast lanes
mew and *screek* and *scrawk* halloo.

Oily birds of lake and high tarn
snapping midges from the eddies;
navigators of the ditchlands;
webfoots of the swamp and fenland;
longtoes of the meadow grasses
black or white or speckle-winged.

All the tribes that track the weather
round the globe on proven circuits
over oceans and landmasses,
craning oboe necks in chorus –
join the V, the flying delta,
sing my song of featherlution.

Come and hear a canny guru
crested all in nous and know-how
sideways, downward, upward mobile.

Picket all the corporate glaciers,
zoot along now, join the movement.
Iamb iamb, dactyl dactyl,
spondee spondee, anapest,
trochee trochee, pyrrhic pyrrhic
sing Big-Cuckoo-in-the-Clouds.

2. Peisthetaerus to the Birds

When Love rutted with Chaos
they made the coloured eggs of you.
Before Zeus could *gaga* his Logos,
you tested the Godless sky.

You still have wings, but you're brought low.
Friends, you peck the crumbs of Man.
He thinks 'bird-brained' means 'mental';
he nails you for food and fun.

Even churches are spiked and wired.
For every bird table there's an air-gun;
for every reserve, a battery farm.
Free range isn't 'out of range'.

Dignity? You're caught and sold;
plucked and gutted and cling-filmed:
Kieved or Kormad or Fricasseed,
no gravy brings you dignity.

Don't blunt your beaks on concrete.
A banquet on every street or square?
You'll be pecking a brother or sister
from beer and take-away spew.

3. Take Advantage Business Group *to the Birds*

Do you know how humans rave
about *Big-Cuckoo-in-the-Clouds?*
    Until now our alphas drank
like fat fishes in the City bars;
    our hotties starved themselves
for little Gucci dresses.
    Now they've all turned twitcher:
they're pan-scanning you lot for tips!

    Up with the Lark and all day
busy busy clapping their Bills –
    bills of impeachment, I mean.
They flock with lawyers to the courts,
    brooding their grievances;
hatching their cocky plots and schemes.
    They've even taken to naming
each other after you birds:

    I met a columnist with
an ulcer branded 'The Grouse';
    a Landlord's Agent tenants
call 'The One-Eyed Crow';
    and then there's that dapper
party Leader – 'The Quail' – who winces
    whenever you mention
his coalition with 'The Goose'.

It's spreading to the names
of our real pride and joy – the Car:
        now it's *Osprey*; soon we'll have
Nighthawks, Popinjays and *Wrens*.
    We'll be climbing over
ourselves to shop in your cloud-malls,
        clamouring for wings, talons;
any chance to accessorize.

    Without land rents or tax,
you can nappy your chicks with cash.

Shoal

Mid July.   After last orders, Jim,

the gardener at Dove Cottage, is recruiting

a bunch of us to walk around the lake.

The hot moon swells. Some of us are hungry

for the big hush, where the night is rich with earth

and smoke and starlight – like our whiskies.

Jim shepherds us down to a gravelly beach.

Hill-slopes inch close and loom. He is showing

us a wonder, throwing fistfuls of stones

high into darkness above cool, still water.

They hang, then fall, plinking a shoal of notes

on impact – the plainsong of weight,   or gravity.

The Tonic

'Wild Garlic', I'd have it,
'can you smell it?'
        I scooped the stream
        then offered you
        that tonic
        so you drank,
        savouring its tang.
Upstream, you heard
flies bickering
on a baking carcass –
claggy froth
breaking down
into fizz.
        Through those eyes
        and teeth
        our stream
        had slummed,
        licking at its lips
        before it ran.

The Lake in the Trees

You were late –
        but I knew
        you were coming
as I listened
        for your reverb
        on the cobbles.
I get so close
        to thinking I'm locked
        out of this life,
when openly
        it's glittering
        off the sheen
of the highest,
        greenest leaves,
        and the miracle
is a lake, a sea,
        lifted into the arms
        of the trees
by a faith
        that can only
        take hold
in this light.

Under Orion, Midsummer

Leaving
      the Britannia
for Elterwater
      Common,
we'd let our posse
      drift ahead.

There it was:
      my glow worm –
a smouldering
      comma
between our talk
      and first
tentative
      kiss.

When I slipped you
      the seed of this
at work
      how like you
to scold me
      for skewing
your artfully groomed
      poise
with glow worms,
      stars.

Two Fugitives

When we bailed out
of that dance
we weren't quite lovers,
just fugitives
taking care no one
was following
as we darted
past each streetlamp's
net of light.

It was almost black
as we climbed our perch
above White Moss
and I lit that bent cigar
and smoked the midges
off our hair and skin.

If there were stars
I can't remember –
only that you sat
behind me, close,
your arms pillion
around my chest
as we rode
dark space
before us.

The Tang

Barely
a   pulse
between
flash
and   thunder
you return
from
the storm
and   desire
is the
           taste
and   tang
of tingling
           electrons
ferried
by   rain
and caught
on
your   skin.

Punch

Easedale Tarn in June.
> You in first,
>> kicking land away –
>>> me combing the shore
>> before following.
> What made me
swim out so far
> and eel-dive
>> under?
>>> This was before
>> I'd read about
> strata of cold
in tarn water
> that stop the heart.
>> Something spooked me
>>> down there – burst
>> my held breath
> in one sucker punch.
When I surfaced –
> eyes and mouth
>> opening
>>> to air and light –
>> my skull
> was a ping-pong ball
on wide-open sea.

Glad Tidings

You shielded
eyes
and scanned
the headway.
The swell
was lakewater
chrome
from Seahouses
to the Farne
Islands.
Airborne Puffins
hung
orange flippers
over
blur-reflected
wings –
skimming each
flicker.
As they veered
and shrank,
I trawled
the soda-stream
wake
where our own slow
passage
was sheening
over.

Trig Points

Clock-tick, birdsong, cars.
My palate wakes from last night:
whisky, wood smoke, stars.

This morning, no wind.
Chimney smoke climbs heavenwards –
a direct statement.

Yesterday (pressure
low) it dawdled all over –
agenda hidden.

A breeze sweeps the trees.
The lightshow on my table
small change of a star.

A leaf turns over
its green days on the stem, leaps –
pioneers the air.

A widening gulf
between the glossy berry
and the falling leaf.

High wind. The branches
seem to be beckoning in
a harsher regime.

                                    The spines of nettles,
                         though bent so far, will recoil,
                                    lash out at the air.

Lit coals crack and fly.
Later, dim, they'll give nothing
to their next of kin.

Airplane, satellite,
meteor shower – tonight
the sky goes too far.

On the perfectly
lateral branch, three blackbirds –
three semi-quavers.

An electric fence
sparks in the rain. Thirteen cows
in reflective trance.

Sun on Dunmail Raise.
One sheep ahead of the flock,
kneeling to the grass.

                              Where mud is deepest
                        the traces of man and beast
                              are one and the same.

The way moss makes one
the tree and the dry stone wall,
imperceptibly.

Look in a puddle –
we're all there: the water, clay,
a transfer of sky.

A turning canoeist –
paddle almost a backhand
returning the light.

Thickening its ranks
this deluge beats down even
the smoke's uprising.

The river bears leaves
(brown, gold) in sure procession –
the lit bed their shades.

                                        A line of stepping
                                stones – seventeen syllables
                                overwhelmed by flood.

At the weir, the lake's
near perfect composure frays –
water shows its teeth.

On grey days like this,
gusts of wind rub at the lake
but can't get a shine.

A lone cobweb hangs
from the campsite tap – supports
one obese droplet.

On the edge of sleep
I'm startled by the night rain
losing its own beat.

A premonition:
hailstones pelt down my chimney,
sign the rug in soot.

Now in the coal shed –
things I want out of the way,
can't bear to let go.

Chimney-smoke merging
into the slow lapse of light.
When does Autumn end?

The Grate

And we packed and left:
you to Wimbledon,
me to Crossgates;
> our bed was stripped,
> our wine-stained carpet
> salted and scrubbed.
Back then
everything we owned
could fit in one car.
> Clouds burst their valves
> hosing Fairfield,
> rinsing White Moss Common
> and every rounded stone
> that drew our heat
> or felt our weight
> arrive, depart.
I waited for my lift
and pictured you tense
at your wheel,
fixing your glasses straight
mile by sloshing mile
as I sat and counted
rain-shots down the flue
onto embers
I'd not yet shovelled;
> ashes I'd almost tipped
> into my writing case;
and would unpack now
on this grate of breath.

The Navigators

———(11

'But you cannot compare a river with a road,
because roads belong to history and rivers to geography.

And so?

Men do not make history: they endure it as they endure geography.
And history, anyhow, is all a matter of geography.'

The Little World of Don Camillo, Giovanni Guareschi

'O build your ship of death, for you will need it.'

'The Ship of Death', D.H. Lawrence

'The past isn't dead. It isn't even past.'

William Faulkner

The Sink Hole

We were hauling coal back to Rotherham
on t' Dearne and Dove. It were past midday.
New Year. Frost had made a permanent home
in the trees, and a skin of ice gave way

as Jack and me lugged our boat for'ard.
Mist were ganging around. You couldn't see
up or down that long canal. It were hard:
we were slipping and sliding, and hardly

seeming to make a whit o' real progress.
Rope agin our nithered hands were cruel,
but our toes agin our boots were worse.
Force all but wrestled us into t' canal

when it happened. Suddenly, summat wild
were sucking our boat back towards Barnsley:
that canal were spooked and buckin' its load –
like t' Devil had radged it. Jack and me

were helpless as Gert shouted me name
from out in t' mist. But it were over
sharp as it began. When t' fit had gone
our boat rested, holed and creaking under

its load. Bed were dry. We were fast there
for weeks. Pit shaft had swallowed t' canal
just less than a field back. Any closer
and this story wouldn't be ours to tell.

Ballad of the Wandering Navvy

Paddy sailed from County Cork
 and worked as hard as any;
hungry Mancs and Tykes joined ranks
 and kicked his poor skull empty.

So if you are an Irishman
 you'd better find another,
'cos when the tempers rise again,
 you'll need to stick together.

The clergy call us apes and drunks
 and say we have no souls;
but souls don't get the diggin' done,
 and souls don't lay canals.

They call our women fallen girls
 because we do not marry,
though marriage is for settled folk
 and not your rovin' navvy;

unwelcome when his job is done,
 he tramps from town to town –
and trampin's not for womenfolk
 with kiddies trailin' on.

Drink a toast then to each lass
 good enough to have us;
we've got no charms or uniforms,
 just spades and moleskin britches.

The engineers and businessmen
  take all the cash and glory;
they use us worse than donkeys –
  and never need say sorry.

Some jobs will pay you by the day,
  and most jobs by the yard;
but some jobs pay you of a piece,
  and then the wranglin's hard,

'cos if you form a butty gang
  and share and share alike,
you'd better keep up with the best,
  be you strong or weak.

I'll give it to you straight and true
  as any dug canal;
although his life is hard and short,
  a navvy's proud as hell;

and if he kips in shanty-huts
  and glugs a hefty ration,
a navvy's is the brawn and guts
  that builded up this nation.

So stand in line and bend your back,
  and let your shovel fall;
'cos if you can't dig long and fast,
  you'd best not dig at all.

The Wheat Horse

We used a pub above one of t' locks.
I took this mare of ours into t' stables
and there were a black in t' next box:
half starved, and stood on three legs.

I went to Dad, and he saw its owner
in t' pub. 'It's lame, so I'm sending it
to t' knacker's', bloke said. Now whether
dad took pity on that beast, he got it

plus five quid in exchange for our mare.
You can get locked up, working a boat
with a lame beast, so we sneaked out o' there
while it were still dark. Come daylight

we let that horse graze 'til after nightfall.
It were a long trip. Horse were near dead
but it slogged on, like it were grateful.
I took it straight over to Bingley's yard

when we got back. He shod its good feet
and cut all t' bad stuff off t' other one.
Dad put a pint of wheat on t' stove, boiled it
wi' watter; put it in t' beast's nose-tin.

Ten year that horse gave us, hauling wheat.

Attercliffe

Three piece suites, old mattresses, bedsteads,
dead dogs, kittens, tyres. You name it,
they chucked it down the cutting. Old hands
would load up a heavy iron boat
two inches down by the head, and then run
at half throttle to stop all the clutter
fouling the prop. One of Furley's men
stripped a gearbox running over a cooker.
When we passed under bridges, folk spat
at us, or sometimes worse. It were a rude
stretch. We kept bilge-water in a bucket
on deck, so, when they spat down one side,
we'd chuck our mucky stuff over t' other.
A fair exchange, I say, water for water.

Harker's *Michael H*

Rotherham wasn't such a lucky town
for Harker's *Michael H*. Back in thirty-one
the river flushed that boat over the weir
and pinned it to the arch of Chantry Bridge.
It's no small thing, going down a weir,
but getting up again, well, that's like
calling in favours from a man in his grave.
Even when the river settled back down
they were forced to flood the near empty hold
before that boat would fit under the bridge.
It was converted into a dry cargo barge,
and ran, up and down, from Rotherham mill,
but was holed, back in fifty-six, running
over stolen safes dumped in the canal.
The safes were empty (no prizes for guessing),
whilst the hold of the *Michael H* was full.

Slow Days are Gone Days

Under the bridges and into the towns,
bailing and throwing out scraps to the swans,
out on the water,
home days.

Rotherham, Swinton, Doncaster, Goole,
then on the Humber and cruising to Hull,
right to the sea days,
great days.

Hauling the coal and the sugar and grain,
loading the boat and unloading again,
scrubbing the deck down,
slog days.

Horsepower, engine-power, man-power too,
whatever power it took to get through,
at 2 miles-an-hour,
slow days.

Winding hole,
turn us round,
winding hole,
reel back time.

Dry days and wet days and better days come,
mild days and hot days and bitter days go,
wind in the face days,
tan days.

Confidence, Kingfisher, Forward and *Swift,*
Valiant, Victory, Progress and *Sheaf,*
The Humber Princess,
boat days.

Air-ways and railways and motorways pay
faster than waterways, draining away,
slow days are gone days,
these days.

Closing the lock gates and leaving the towns,
bailing and throwing out scraps to the swans,
taking in water,
gone days.

In the 70s

You'd fall in
the canal
and surface –
a tiny leech
behind your ear
like an implant
translating
the shivers
of perch
right through
your flesh.

Jasmine

Part One

My granddad – my mother's dad – built a boat.
After he retired he built a cabin-cruiser
in the back garden of his council house.

He'd spent his last working years bartering
and acquiring by mysterious means
all the raw materials he needed –

plywood, fibreglass, engine parts, glue,
even a chemical toilet. So when he retired
the business became a second lease of work

to ferry him on. He called his boat *Jasmine*.
The word included a letter from each
of our family's names. I remember

him stencilling it onto the prow
one summer afternoon in the seventies,
after it had been lowered down to moor

amongst water-beetles and petrol-rainbows.
With its rectangle cabin and snub nose,
it bulked like no other boat on the canal,

something that would outlast us all.
Not a barge. Not a fly-boat. A heavy
box-boat. *Jasmine*, the Churchill Tank boat.

*

My granddad's boat had more than one engine.
First, an inboard tangle of pipes and valves –
assembled out of parts from deceased machines.

He seemed always to be tightening its bolts –
or loosening. It gave him a lasting odour
somewhere between *Swarfega* and engine-oil.

Then, out of the blue, he let it die; fitted
a more powerful outboard almost overnight,
and from then on, the inboard never happened.

My sister and I were wary, at first,
of venturing on deck without life jackets.
We were happier inside, playing cards,

sitting amongst our Nana's horse-brasses,
or tuning in the black and white TV
as the wakes of other boats tripped our balance.

When I was first coaxed up behind the wheel,
I gripped it like a handrail. With my granddad
standing close by my side, egging me on

and cranking up the engine, I imagined
our own wake unsettling cygnets and coots;
swamping low banks of primrose and wild garlic.

Part Two

Then the years churn. My granddad has decided
   to sell his boat. He's seventy-five.
He's had two strokes and lost his wife to cancer.

   The upkeep of a boat is too much
for him. Too much pumping. Too much bailing.
   So he's decided Jasmine must be sold –

and for less than the cost of a funeral.
   She'll be passed on to a couple from Leeds:
the man has a moss of damp beard, smokes roll-ups,

   and his wife is quiet, but with a way
of looking right at me when she listens
   to what I say, as if she understands.

I'm twelve or thirteen, and aggressively
   shy. When she looks at me in her way
on that summer afternoon on my granddad's

   boat, I know what it is I have to do.
I've got to help him hand our *Jasmine* over.
   I'll go with them to open the locks

and swing bridges; throw out or catch the towline.
   I want to sit up on the cabin roof,
and glance her face as tall trees scatter sunlight.

*

It's the last swing-bridge before Leeds. I leap
off the boat and onto the tow-path. Moving
 with confidence, now, I unlock the bridge,

and nudge it from its stasis with my shoulder,
 feel it swing almost weightless on its pin.
I look back at the boat and make my signal

 for them to rev the engine and come through.
There's my granddad, gripping the wheel and speaking,
 as she looks on ahead. I clock her face

as they pass. She looks at me. Her expression –
 how can I describe it? Her eyes are hard:
her mouth has pursed as if on something bitter;

 I wish I could check it again. I wish
I'd a photo. I'd lay it on the table
 and list the things that ended with that look.

On the way home, Granddad gives me a fiver.
 'Here', he announces, 'they've given you this.
I told them you only came for the money

 so they've given you this'. It's the first
fiver I've ever pocketed. I'm gutted.
 But not gutted enough to give it back.

Ellipses

I'd enter summer in a rowing boat
my granddad towed behind his larger craft;
my nana used it picking raspberries
and wildflowers on banks without access
and sometimes when we'd moored up for the night
and I was left to take it after tea
I'd row and row and build a rhythm up
for when a faster, broader boat pressed by
and rock and ride the choppy waves of wake
until the surface stilled itself again
and then I'd let the boat just spin or drift
and lift the oars from out of water's clutch
so they could dab and drip their ellipses
between the heavy brackets of each bank…

The Passage

The thought of sleeping on my granddad's boat
would tie a little reef knot in my gut
in case it might be true what my cousin said
about the earwigs squeezed in every nook
that scaled your neck and face when you dozed off
and crawled into your ears and eyes and mouth.
It's true that when you bed down on a boat
you feel a little closer to each pulse
that ripples through the never-ceasing world –
and then you lie awake and listen hard
to every slosh or knock against the hull
from rats and water voles you've read about,
or sniping owls who probe and tense the dark.
And then you feel the press and seethe of cold
from water leaking through each seam or joint;
the dreams that chase your ebbing into sleep
are full of rain and water rising up
to flush you down the cellar of a lock.
But somehow the little plywood fort
is proof enough against the flood of doubt;
the hatch you close at night against the gnats,
you open in the morning to the light.
There's a photo of my mum's somewhere
of me with one leg on the boat, one off,
as if I'm not sure, now, where I belong
and nothing in my face gives it away
except at some remove I'm still absorbed
and at a stretch no boy can hold for long.

'Earthquake felt across much of UK...'

A man suffered a broken pelvis
when masonry collapsed on his bed.

    Under the canal bridge, one brick
    scattered its own reflection.

A bubble rose from the water
into the bulls-eye of a floating tyre.

    The moon-face on the winding hole
    laughed to itself for a second;

the mooring ropes of barges
picked up signals in Morse.

    One crack scrawled a long signature
    across the lock keeper's house.

27 February 2008

Winding Hole

Where, once, the *Sheaf*, the *Swift* and the *Humber Princess*
turned their slow circles on this acre of water,
now, a swan and her train of seven bustling cygnets
wear on their feathers a cargo of dew and pollen
brushed from Foxgloves, Willowherb and Red Campion.

Mexborough Quad Bandits

i.

Who are these
mucky sandy boys
ruddy faces
riding quadbikes;

wasprevs
spitting against birds
and river
wisps of sound.

Step wide aside
as they plough footpath furrows
up bank down
winding up their swarm
until
they veer and cough
in gritty fallow
stubble fields
of dust.

ii.

Fat treads mill
as the lead bike trails dust tunnels
for the quad tribe
to breathe and ride;

crosswind
cuts into revs
that bite and hurl
meringue
of topsoil
east.

iii.

Dragonflies retreat
      as quad banditos
   rodeo whoop;

  thigh and calf
   tensing boys
    big up
   fuck you exhaust
    against
wind's outbreath
  sigh of yellow rape
   and poppy crimson
    dusk.

Canal Surf

You nick a windlass
        off a moored boat
to open the gate.
One of you needs to crank
        the sluice
fast as owt
        while the rest
tread water in front.
Waiting for that two-ton truck
        of gush
makes me hard,
and when I twist and ride
        the wave push
I almost come.
You'll hear dry fucks
        nagging about cold cramps,
hidden hazards,
and fucking Weil's disease,
        but this isn't
for your mum.
Keep your bottle
        and your mouth shut
and it's adrenalin
Jager Bomb
        for free.

Flood Risk

Crosswinds

blowing

pipes

on Dearne

sluice-gates

are

breath

mother gave

and flood

sucked back.

Brigand

I switch off the revs,
pop my ears from the helmet's pod,
and blink white lines from my sight.
I crunch along the footpath
to a hide on Denaby Ings.
A bird I can't name
trills like a rag on soapy glass –
a squeak with a chime in it.
Coots chafe like chair legs on lino;
a dove chants a wood mass.
There are water take-offs,
and water landings –
a lush trawl of sound.
Wing beats ripple
and a gull throttles its cry
on obsessive/compulsive loop.
A jay flits a toy windmill
in and out through the slats;
ducks squeeze their honks
then hush.
This is the moment I love –
when two minutes' silence
is a slow pull of Moonshine.
It's interrupted by gnats
teasing at the edge of buzz
and the clatter and creak
is me donning my helmet
and wrapping this up.

Mexborough, Water-Fronted Properties Released

scaffolding
                on anchored
        new-builds
                thrills
    in the wake
                of the Humber
        Princess

*

                methane-nudged
        ripples
                frame
    blue-green
                dragonfly biplanes
    dogfighting
                mirror

*

slow perch
            rise and taste
    meniscus
            where
pollen phlegms
            on diesel
        slicks

*

                    sunken
                            bubble-wrap
                    swaps
                    silver
            for croc-skin's
                            deep
                    algal green

                    *

feathers
            and blossom
        pink
            the grass –
        one
            with nectar
    the other
            blood

                    *

                the flat
            ceiling
                of Pasture
    Road Bridge
                is larval
        with light

                    *

shoaling carp

        ten

    times ten:

          whisks

               scrambling

            yolk

       of sun

        *

               roped

      packing bales

              comprise

       a settee-raft

               where three

        pink princes

              drift

       and read sky

        *

pup-yapping

          George-flying

    lawns

        backing up

   to canal

       surrender

  to swans

        *

the willow
          is a skull
where neurons
               are reflected
     light
               dreaming
          rain

          *

          at the bleed-off
     a scab
               of twigs,
crab-apples
               and polystyrene
          clots
               in vain

          *

a grass snake
               thickens water's
     sinew:
               a wake-ripple
     taking skin,
               muscle

          *

taut dragonflies
                    skim
          and flirt –
                    sapphire
          to hook
                    the eye's
          fish

                    *

     cut
               grass
          khakis
                    sluggish
rheumy canal
                    falling back
          on lock

                    *

          willows
                    collapse,
               but
                    scent
     of open water
                    is bankable,
               rich

ANGLERS REQUIRE PERMITS

An upside-down shed
crowns
this dumpsite.
    Smoky char
    coarsens
    breath.

A mugged fridge,
broken like a safe;
    tree cuttings
    forgetting sap,
fibreglass
shedding form
and function.

    A sofa
    spilling foam
    is cindered
    toffee.
Clinkers
and rusted wire
thistle
the scorch.

    Here,
    white, silky ash
    is barren
    as light.

Mexborough Bridge S2

      Yesterday
teenagers launched
a blue paddling pool liferaft
      on the canal –
crowding the towpath
like revellers
on a ferry going   down.

They tipped themselves
      shrieking
in twos and threes –
girls maintaining
beehives above water,
boys shedding   trunks.

      Today
I read their signatures:
sheath-like *Mr Freeze* wrappers;
BOOST tins;
Marlborough Blue;
      two
      puckered
salmon-pink
      socks
and a pair of shorts
lining serrated   with nettles.

Darkhouse

across cliffs
of brick
a cine film
of idling
light

under
the high
winch roof
jellied reflections
shiver
and tense

walkways
crumble into
drink

sealed-up
windows
lock space
bankrupt
and warehousing
dark

The Edge

Is a kid
 climbing out
  of the canal –
   a scar
    from his
     right hip to
      his left
       nipple
        that folds
         like
          the lip of
          a barge's
          wake.

Dunn Street: Abandoned Lock

Geese slice
            carpets
of bile-green algae –
                their trails
        are veins
            in stilton.

A purple fit ball
                baggy
        as an afterbirth
                chafes against
        coke tins.

Up this infected
            cut
        wader birds
                tiptoe
    crisp packets
            and chip tray
        rafts.

They peck
            the foetor,
        tapping
            for reflex.

When They Next Make You Redundant

You might try to think of your life
poised at the steer of a barge
where canal steps down to the Don
and lock gates unlatch and infold.
Imagine the trip in your blood:
as you gaze at river ahead
and the cautious nose of your barge
sniffs then drifts into the flow,
you feel the current take grip.
The barge is plugged into a mains
so all you can do from this point
is solder your fist to the steer,
and amp up your savvy to match.

And amp up your savvy to match,
solder your fist to the steer:
all you can do from this point
as the mains strums through the hull
is welcome the current's intent
and churn then speed into the bend
with the hungry nose of your barge.
When you glance at river behind
savour the burn in your blood
as lock gates inch back and close
and the Don sweeps on from canal.
Primed at the steer of your barge,
you'll rise and breathe in this life.

The Tug

i.m. Mary and Ted Bedford

The old man walking a dog on the tow path
  could be my granddad, and the dog, a vexed,
greasy peke, or Shih Tzu, could be my nana's.

  On the boat she'll rise and tweak the heat
on a pan of stewing steak, not for Granddad
  but for the dog, Tina. Before too long

she'll be convincing her opposite number
  on the cruiser next door that a night's kip
would be a fine thing what with Ted's snores filling

  and quaking the berth like a knackered-out tug
stepping up its knots through the Standage Tunnel.

Long weeds

        trail
   the Don;
         floating
      bouquets
           of tiny-petalled
     flowers
         where summer
      throws
        the current
   silver coin.

Cave Time and Sea Changes

'Yes! Very funny this terrible thing is. A man that is born falls into a dream like a man who falls into the sea. If he tries to climb out into the air as inexperienced people endeavour to do, he drowns – nicht wahr?... No! I tell you! The way is to the destructive element submit yourself, and with the exertions of your hands and feet in the water make the deep, deep sea keep you up. So if you ask me – how to be?'

Lord Jim, Joseph Conrad

'No shore is without its Homeric echoes. It is one of the realms of the heroes, the giant zone of liminality between land and sea, the sphere of chance-in-play. Outcomes are never certain there.'

The Mighty Dead: Why Homer Matters, Adam Nicolson

'to name the rocks
is to navigate
successfully among them'

Yellow & Blue, Thomas A. Clark

Staithes

For C.G.

This place needs all the shelter it can raise.
We're up on the cliffs in a gale force.
The full moon's a spotlight. Cloud-shadows
are stampeding over fields and barn roofs,

driven over cliffs like cattle into open sea.
Below us, breakers go berserk around
lumps of fallen coast, churning wakes of veined
and marbling foam. Drunk on adrenalin, we

run with the wind at our backs. Inland,
big trucks roll over by Scaling Dam;
where moorland wind breaks into the open
whatever it snatches won't hope to land,

least not unscathed. This is why we came
to this edge of things. From turned-up TVs,
smooth voices warn the flock to stay indoors,
but we've broken cover, only ourselves to blame.

Our Love is a Whalebone

i.

        We launched
    our bellies
          against the break
     and roll
       of surf;
     or   tumbled under,
      came up
          spitting salt
and God knows what
            back into Atlantic.

     We pried
           oracles of rock pools
    for life;
       felt molluscs
  suck down
      onto rock.

As noon drew steam
         from wet sand,
   we breathed
      the spliff
 of baked wrack,
       and salt
  sweated home
      to our tongues.

ii.

On the path
to Baggy Point
the bleached
whalebone
and its legend
did nothing
to explain
why those giants
resign bone and blubber
to flies,
who once
trawled open jaws
through fizzing
pastures of krill.

iii.

I saw love
        in two canoeists
snail-pacing
          around
    headland –
        rocked
in each breath
         as ocean
    exhaled
      into coast.

iv.

It was the cliff
and
questions
lobbied
by the edge.

You wanted him more,
but not
salt
of the words.

Natural
that we slept
soon after.
Enough
to feel
stalks
prickle
my belly;
fret
cooling whale-bones
under
my aching
calves.

Counting Stones
For E.B.

i.

Although he's nine,
        your son
would test slugs
        and ants
on his tongue;
        take a playful leap
off the cliff.

Carrying a stone
        the size of his skull
he'd wade out,
        fully clothed
into the tide,
        and hurl that stone
for breakers
        to volley back.

There's no danger
        in his brain.
Without your voice,
        your arms,
he'd ride the pogo
        in his spine
against surges
        rinsing his prints
from sand.

ii.

Waves swab
the sea wall
      or lick
landing cobbles
for their meal
of chip trays
and grease.

We've met
old friends
of yours here.
They've walked
coast to coast
and next will try
for a child.

You only want
to charm them
with each joy
they have in store,
but your boy
will have none of it.

With waves
      so close
he must touch
and taste them;
useless to hold
him back.

iii.

Today
you're a mollusc
      and we're
squawking gulls.

You draw
your shell down
      tight
and suck.

Your clever
daughter and I
      are picking you
Sea Campions
from the cliff.

She charges inclines
      headlong,
never losing
her footing.

I step away
and count each stone
      she kicks
down.

iv.

On this crescent
       of sand
I keep score.
       Two years
before her cancer
       your mum
takes guard,
       then slogs
clean out
       of the middle
and coins
       this.
The ball lands
       in rocks
where your son
       stands apart;
palms muffed
       over ears,
and doesn't
       try to field.

v.

One more bay
you tell us
as Ravenscar
inches close.

Every mile
we walk,
I answer,
we have to
walk back.

Your daughter
stops asking, now,
and your boy
can hike forever.

Even I'm
learning
            not
to question.

A tall child
in each hand,
you make a V
            together:
those children
are your wings.

Chalk

i.

Chalk cliffs are wax-white and gull-white
sluiced and soiled with thickening mudslides
packed and shattering calcium strata
micro-strata within macro-strata
sunken alcoves and brittle balconies
trauma-warped and trauma-fractured
rich in crevices mortared and pasted
chalk-bleached grasses stitching the crack-face.
Under the ramparts pebbles and obols
treasure-troves spilling bi-valves and bird-skulls
slick as sealskin when the sea licks them
wash and backwash rolling and tonguing
grinding and sucking them down to slivers
breaking and spitting its broken teeth.

ii.

Remember how I brought you the chalkstone
no smooth oval prize laid by the sea-goose
no worry-ball cool in the palm and blue-tinted
a mangled discus cavity-infested
holed like a cheese or a salt-brittle pumice
brown-stained a little and smelling of sea-rot
cavitied cavities mazes in mazes
where whiskery sea-lice furbish their hovels
a heart-stone a brain-stone pitted with losses
clogged with near indigestible flotsam
iodine-treated inside the chambers
pick it up now and shake up its history
its shanty of sand and broken shell-shards
choking and rattling inside its lung.

iii.

Let me cast you as a tall thin chalk-stack
white sea-cavalry charging your buttress
gnawing and thinning the whittled foundation
cut off but in sight from the crumbling mainland.
One of those ruins infested with gull-kind
making a bedlam of airspace above it
where angels and harpies jostle for place.
I'll cast myself as a marginal chalk-pool
slippery weed-slime around my portal
stones of these words gargling inside it
each one rubbing the grain of the other.
A near-empty socket a terrible bodhrǎn
stretched under churn of gravelly breakers
still and mute when the swell falls back.

The Fates

For E.B.

i.

All the blame that's passed between us
can't be unsaid, now, or taken back.
Walking from the South Landing by road
I passed a van as it cruised into a gull.
The van applied its brakes and the gull
tried to lift itself free, but neither act
would save anything. The verdict is clear:
by these tiny margins fates are sealed.
As the gull lies twitching in the road –
a mop-head of feathers and broken bone –
the driver reverses tenderly through
his own trajectory, as if he's sure
he can erase the damage inch by inch.
It holds him: unable to help or move on.

ii.

More and more I question my own judgement.
I've sat here above the North Landing
for half an hour and still don't feel certain
if the tide is advancing or retreating.
The gaps between clouds are widening
but those clouds grow darker and darker.
The morning is redeemed and ruined
in equal measure. Between the shoreline
and the far horizon a cobble is slowly
changing direction. Someone in deep water
is visibly struggling. Who was it
warned me against drawing conclusions?
The souls who look like they're drowning
might well be on the brink of learning.

Cave Time and Sea Changes

For Ruth Palmer

1. History Song

Flamborough, meaning 'Place of Flame', or 'Flame Tower';
  in the Anglo Saxon: 'Flean', 'arrow head',
aiming its barb over sea towards Denmark;

  a chalk tower, a watch tower; vigil to guard
against Longships stirring smoke on the eddies;
  soft tongue of sand and incisor of stack;

a fog-horn; a lighthouse, now without keeper,
  seeding the darkening acres with light;
two landings; a lifeboat and coastguard station

  from which, as August kindles into storm,
the night-watch view lightning strafing the cliff-face
  and ninety tons of chalk slumps into black.

2. August 1974

Tizer of light on the oven-plate sea
as you kneel and bury a toy fire engine
  in the sand. You follow a squat, fat dog

as it nips the heels of surf, get distracted
  by a couple smoking outside a cave.
There you find seagull feathers on the surface

  of a pool, dip your hand and lick the salt
from your chalky fingers. Your dad is calling
  and calling your name: you hear and don't hear

as you tug a weed – a belt of tan leather –
  and thrash it on rock. You taste your own salt
when you can't unearth that buried fire engine.

3. August 1979

You are stood on the beach at the North Landing –
  sun-toasted shingle biting your soles –
watching your mum row out a rubber dinghy,

  her back to the open sea, bobbing close
to the rocks on the jaw of the bay, further
  and smaller. You keep looking at your dad

as he stands by and stares with a scrutiny
  no-one else sees, until the speck that is Mum
loses more and more in her outmatched battle

  with the tide. A muscle clenches your guts.
It keeps clenching; even after the cobble
  throws Mum a line and tows her back to size.

4. After Homer, Odyssey Book V

A brute wave carried him against the rocks
where his flesh would've been flayed, his bones shattered
  had not Athena then inspired his limbs

so he gripped the rock face in desperation
  and clung: but the backwash of the same wave
plucked and flung him far into open ocean –

  as an octopus is flushed from its nook
and pebbles stick in its tentacle's suckers
  so the fingers that gripped the rock were skinned.

Now the heaving waters covered him over
  and there great Odysseus would've drowned
had not Athena lent him premonition.

5. *August 1976*

Walking these cave pools without Mum or Dad
feels like passing through a stadium tunnel
  towards a mass and cymbal-clash of sea

never tested before. Pursed anemones
  nipple pool-rims – plump and wet-liver brown.
You have slipped out of your shoes at the threshold

  and eased your way in touch by touch. Your eyes
have to adjust for slant light to rekindle
  on still-wet chalk. Your bare feet love this cold;

bolts of it flush out the sleep from your muscles.
  Alert in the young timber of your shins,
you pick up a stone and fence with the breakers.

6. Memory Song

Memory shifts in us like a thunderstorm
  moving up a coastline, slowly at first,
dragging shadow and deluge over wind farms;

  advancing vastly on harbours and ports
where jet-skis and kayaks turn tail for shelter.
  We feel safe and detached from where we stand –

miles off at first, until, unexpectedly,
  a coastguard helicopter hammers past
and that storm front is suddenly attacking,

  pelting rock pools and beach sand with shot.
Now the lazy sand flies kick off and scatter
  and we inhale as lightning cracks its whip.

7. August 2010

The cave is the size of a parish church.
You enter the vestibule like a pilgrim
  and address the water as it gulps back

or sighs forward, swell by swell. Sea is traction
  engineered by the drag of sun and moon,
and its heaved weight has quarried out this barrow.

  Greens and ochres and cobalts ink the walls,
but offer no windows of light, no icon.
  Your mania was stilled here in these pools.

You'd almost forgotten your slow approaches
  to the sloshing cave mouth. Those seagull flocks
were grace notes rising from new-scored horizon.

8. History Song

The sea off the headland culls many souls:
in this year Seventeen Ninety Four *twenty*
* fishermen perished in a single storm*

and not one family in the whole village
* escaped the chant of dust to dust*
or did not face an empty chair at supper.

* The wonder remains: whether by the force*
of custom or habitual acquaintance
* with the punching breakers that swamp and drown,*

no survivor abandoned net and cobble;
* all continued to rise and venture forth*
as if no husband ever lost this wager.

9. July 2011

You stumble with your lover to the cave
and, resting at the cliff-face, point out strata
   of livid flesh-tones shining in the rock

as if chalk were evolving vital organs.
   When laid out under your feet they are maps
of ocean depth and ocean treasure rendered

   in concentrations of sapphire and green.
You trip and the gull-cliff rouses in panic:
   a featherless chick plummets from a nest

above, and sprawls – beak opening and closing –
   as if mouthing the mantra of this place
in strains lost on the deaf ears of the living.

10. After Homer, Odyssey Book IV

'Show me how to wait for this divinity.
 A god is no quarry for mortal man.'
Menelaus asked. Eidothea answered.

 'When the sun has climbed the crow's nest of noon
the old man of the sea – forever honest –
 will rise up from the salt and nipping waves

and lie down to rest in a chiselled cavern.
 His seals will join him in their grease and heat:
they will slumber and snore there in a huddle,

 blowing off alien smells of the deep.
I'll take you at dawn, when gull-chicks are famished.
 I'll teach you the tricks to snare this old man.'

11. July 2011: 13.40

A pebble in an eddy-pool can drill
cavities in chalk: likewise in memory.
  Four pairs of shoes abandoned on a rock,

at the cool entrance of a key-shaped passage
  through cliff – tide-flooded and murky with weed.
Unwilling to wade through depths it keeps hidden

  you track back and around only to find
your progress cut off again where gannets
  fly their voices in squadrons around nests:

a posse of lads hurtle rocks in salvos
  at the chicks, laughing out loud with each strike.
Your jaw locks tight. A pulse drills at your temples.

12. July 2011: 13.45

Your photo gifts another world entirely,
  Ruth: that passage through cliff has become more
than just a glimpse through a corroded keyhole –

  it reveals the figure of a cowled man;
the opposite of silhouette. A sapphire
  aura illuminates the jagged frame;

above the waist he is one spectral body
  of light; below he is water and rock
and pool-ripples frozen so still they mimic

  ridges in acres of shale. Here he stands:
Proteus, God of cave-time and sea-changes,
  whose oath is a gannet tracking the winds.

After Apollonius

Idas's tongue was a crack of the lash;
and the spat would've flared had not their comrades
  quired a breaker of shouts to douse its flame.
Jason struck his note; and so did Orpheus.

*

He sang of the lost era when earth, sky
and sea were geared together on a single
  wheel. It was conflict made them grind and split.
The stars, moon and sun held their geometry
  but mountains woke and hunched gigantic backs.
With supple Nymphs to oxidize the current,
  streams murmured life into four-legged things.
He sang how, in the beginning, Ophion
  and Eurymone, daughter of the sea,
governed the world from ice-towered Olympus;
  and how their force was crushed by greater force –
Ophion by Cronos and Eurymone
  by Rhea; and how they plumbed like grain ships
into hull-splitting Ocean... Their usurpers
  ruled the happy Titans when Zeus was still
a whelp in his Dictaen cave; long before
  the earthborn Cyclopes gifted him the bolts;
the thunder-lightning that arms his will today.

*

So the song finished.

                     The pure breath and lyre
of Orpheus had ceased their chords together.
  Yet even so, there was no talk or change
from the crew; their heads were frozen in leaning;
  the vanished melody still held their ears.
Such was the charm of Orpheus – the music
  was still playing in their hearts as they mixed
the wine and honey for Zeus's libation;
  as they poured it over the burning tongues,
then wrapped their limbs for sleep;

                          their dreams for sailing.

Afterword
Some notes on constructing *The Navigators*

In *The Faraway Nearby*, Rebecca Solnit writes: 'The self is a patchwork of the felt and unfelt, of presences and absences, of navigable channels around the walled-off numbness'. The same might be said of a book of poems. Some years ago my writing journey had run aground on an island of my own making. I was living in a mouldy flat. I'd resigned from a job that had made me ill. A very important relationship had broken down. I was still struggling with my health, fighting a numbness brought on by absences of my own. One Sunday I tuned into a radio programme called 'Homer's Landscapes', written and presented by Adam Nicolson. In it, Nicolson examined the journey Odysseus made to Hades, where he must feed blood, honey and wine to the ghost of Tiresias, in order to restore to him the gift of speech. Only Tiresias can offer Odysseus the directions he needs to complete his homeward journey. According to Nicolson, it is as if the Greeks believed that the body and taste of these things were essential not only to life, but to language too. This is a metaphor for poetry itself – for any attempt to make absences or abstractions concrete. The ghosts need their blood and honey, otherwise they'll remain silent shadows.

This is why I've chosen to start this collection, *The Navigators*, with a version of this episode of *The Odyssey*. It acts as a kind of prologue to a book that is full of reconstructions: crowded with personal, historical and mythical ghosts. Marooned on my own journey, I needed to consult with them in order to restore my sense of direction. Some of the poems in this book predate poems in *West North East* (Longbarrow Press, 2013), and some of them were written immediately after. One thing that distinguishes them from the poems in my first volume is a broadening of the canvas of time and place. Another is a greater fascination with the flowing element of water, as it moves through both. The collection starts with rain falling in Cumbria. It flows to the South Yorkshire waterways, before arriving at the sea and another scene in another navigational myth from Ancient Greece.

Section 1: *Trig Points*

The collection begins with poems born out of a writing residency at Wordsworth's Dove Cottage. The first drafts were written some 13 years ago. They've been re-drafted many times since – the form just eluding me, until I started experimenting with free and open forms in 2014. I've taken a long time to discover what many poets start with. This sequence chiefly maps my relationship with the landscape, with creatures, and with my companion of that time, C. Cumbria was the glue that held C and me together, and our relationship struggled after we left. It was as if we couldn't agree on a landscape we wanted to share – and so we retreated separately to places closer to our origins. The poems in *Trig Points* also triangulate mental journeys between past, present and projected future. C and I lacked a shared vison of the future, but this doesn't stop the heart wanting to look back at a loved person and a loved place, trying to find embers to carry forward. Time is a cold landscape without these embers. The frame of this section of the book is also haunted by myth and history. There is a recent adaptation of passages from Aristophanes' *The Birds*, and a sequence that touches on events in Kosovo. Many Kosovan refugees settled in Cumbria, and if I go beyond my right to speak of such subjects, I do so in order to remind myself that no idyll is unvisited by voices from worlds outside it. I thought this each time a military jet passed over the Cumbrian sky.

Section 2: *The Navigators*

In 2009 I received a commission to write poems about the history of the South Yorkshire waterways. I'm no stranger to canals. My grandfather had built a canal boat after he retired, and many holidays in my childhood were spent on his cabin-cruiser, navigating the Leeds-Liverpool canal. The commission resulted in some historical monologues in the voices of navvies and boatmen, as well as personal reminiscences of time on my grandfather's boat. In 2013 I moved to Mexborough, in South Yorkshire, and found myself 5 minutes from the canal. There, I navigated the waterways as they are now. On one stretch of the canal, a number of houses back onto the water. From the street, they look like ordinary semis or terraces, but from the canal bank they appear more exotic – the domestic waterfronts decorated with bunting, statues of herons, and with little huts and fishing platforms. Some homes even have boats. There is something exciting, for me, about having a boat at the bottom of the garden. I suppose it is possible to look at the motorcar as Everyman's Argo, parked in the driveway or the street outside every home. But it doesn't work for me. There's something special about a boat – about stepping off land and onto a craft that navigates another element. Any waterway has a mystery that a road can't achieve. When I think of my time on my grandfather's boat, I realise my experiences were a growth. It's more poignant now because I understand how important that new adventure was at the end of my grandparents' lives. Parts of my coming of age and their retirement coincided on the waterways. The canals will always lead back to my history, and to theirs. And they lead back to history with a capital H (or even a dropped one).

Section 3: *Cave Time and Sea Changes*

In 'Reference Back', Philip Larkin said that 'though our element is time, / We are not suited to the long perspectives / Open at each instant of our lives.' All through my life, long perspectives have opened in coastal landscapes. I've returned to the sea for reflection and regeneration, and the poems I've set there are epiphanies that hatch on literal and metaphorical thresholds. This final section explores key moments in three romantic relationships. I've questioned whether there might be something insensitive about placing love poems for three women in such proximity. However, I am interested in the drama of the human heart in time. This is supposed to be one of the things the compass of poetry helps us navigate – look at poems from *Gilgamesh* to Hardy's *Poems of 1912-13* to Hughes' *Birthday Letters*. In this final section I try to construct my own compass. The denouement is a sequence that explores Proustian memories of Flamborough Head, where I attempt to fuse mythical, personal and historical threads in one fugue-like movement. It culminates with a glimpse of the Greek god of sea-changes, Proteus. This is channelled through a photo taken by my partner, Ruth. I use it as a talisman to return me to a present that is never-ending, and always in the wind. The marooned sailor uses it to find a way home, if home is the seat of our affections, or the starting point for all new expeditions.

Epilogue

The book doesn't quite end there. I've chosen to exit with another mythical scene. This time it's a night before Jason and his Argonauts embark on their journey. Jason is losing his nerve. Two of the crew have fallen into bitter dispute. It's almost come to blows, when Orpheus enchants everyone with a song about our elemental origins. The Argonauts carry the song in their hearts long after the music stops, and even into their sleep and dreams. This seemed like the perfect note upon which to suspend my poetic navigations. It's often said that time is problematic in the human mind. We displace the present into the past, or project it into the future. DH Lawrence wrote about his desire to pioneer a poetry of the present – something that eluded even Orpheus in the end, perhaps. Events later in his life led Orpheus to regret the backward look. In another version of his myth, after his dismemberment by the Maenads, his decapitated head is left to float on the river Hebrus – still singing – until it reaches the Mediterranean shore. As Ezra Pound says in 'Exile's Letter', 'there is no end of things in the heart.' This book places my stones on the cairn of that idea.